I0471788

Foreword

Want to start an online business? But not sure how to start the first step?

This book will be your online business guide, taking you through the online business world and what you need to know.

This book will be divided into two parts, the first part will break down everyone's myths about online business, so that you can understand more of what the online business world is like.

The second part will give you a step-by-step understanding of how to build the foundation of an online business, allowing you to start your business with a plan!

Let this book open your business doors to the online world!

Online Business MythBusters

Myth #1: Is Online Business Really That Good?

You must have heard someone say at some point: "Doing an online business is great! It gives me the "perfect life"! It's convenient, I have time freedom, and you can choose to work from home, and even manage your business whilst traveling!" After all... is online business really that good?

I'm sorry, I'm about to break your beautiful fantasy.

I think before you start an online business, have a clear understanding of its pros and cons so that you can plan and prepare before you decide to start.

In the online business world, it is not as beautiful as most people imagined it to be, just like the real business world, the Internet is full of hackers, liars, viruses... If you are not careful, the entire website may be lost, and even customers will be lost due to mistakes. There's also a chance to encounter the loss of money!!

Did you just think: "Well, since the Internet is so "scary", I just shouldn't start it…"

I don't want to scare you, but if we don't know the danger, and we think everything is beautiful and we're never going to make mistakes, I'm sorry to burst your bubble but that is not the case. This is like standing out naked in -30 degrees weather, without any prior plans or research you could get hurt badly.!

Fortunately, today you will find there are many resources available and I will show you how to prepare and plan so you can start your first online business, without going in blindly!

Myth #2: Do people really buy online?

Before you know it, the online world has actually been integrated into our lives. Credit cards, online banking, email, communication software, mobile phones, watching movies, watching TV, ordering takeaways, buying air tickets, and booking hotels all of these exist in our lives. We have been slowly occupied by the Internet.

Truth behold, we will only rely on it more in the future, because we have enjoyed the convenience and speed brought by the online world. It is impossible to go back to the days when we had to wait in line at the bank for bank transactions in the morning or waiting on the phone for several hours just to talk to customer service etc. However, you may still encounter some businesses that are very traditional and still service you in these methods.

Now that the online world has become an integral part of life, this is the reason why you should start an online business today, or you can bring your current brick & mortar business online.

Remember that online business does not give you a "perfect life" (of course, a successful online business could bring about the ideal lifestyle mentioned above). Taking your business online is a **"must need"** direction in the future, just like using credit card collections within your business.

Online business has changed our buying habits. Before anyone buys a product, they will generally want to search for the nearest store on the Internet, or directly find the best and fastest delivery method online to buy.

Taking your business online is a "must need" direction in the future

資料來源: Hootsuite

According to the latest Global Online Report in January 2022, 58.4% of the world's 7 billion people shop online every week.
And with the numbers rising by at least 10% every year, you can imagine that in the future, online businesses will be one of the most common everyday services.

Myth #3: Do you have to be at the forefront of the latest technology?

One of the reasons why many people are hesitant to start an online business is because they feel like: "It is too late to start, and everything is changing on a daily basis and I can't keep up with the latest information and technology, I might as well give up"

You need to keep on top of the latest information and technology in your profession and industry, but in the process of building an online business, you only need to build on a platform that already exists steadily and has a large number of users to start with.

Stop wasting time looking and trying to learn the latest technology and platform, because your ultimate goal is to build an online business in the shortest time possible.

Once you build your first online business platform, then slowly you can learn how to improve it. But because the online world is developing too fast, unless you are in the technology industry, you don't need to use every innovation immediately. You only need to choose a suitable system or platform that allows you to get started immediately.

The advantages of building an online business on a mature platform are:

- **Already has a large number of active users**

- **The system is stable**

- **There are successful testimonials and examples for referencing and learning**

- **You can find professionals on this platform to help**

Myth #4 : Can You Really Start A Business With $0?

You should have heard countless advertisements or friends around you tell you that online business is very simple and can be started without any cost!

Is there really such a thing where you can start without any money down? It sounds like a dream to many!

If it really is zero cost, I believe that many people around you today should be online entrepreneurs or already have online businesses, but in fact they are not.

To do business, whether it is a traditional brick-and-mortar business or an online business, "cost" is necessary. The difference is whether to start a business at high cost or low cost. Online business is the latter. But low cost does not mean zero cost, please keep this in mind.

Whether it is a traditional brick-and-mortar business or an online business, "cost" is necessary.

So what costs do you need to prepare for an online business?

The following is a basic Start Up Checklist for your reference (the price is based on February 2022 as an example) so that you can have a budget in mind to prepare you for an online business.

基本Start Up預算 Checklist

	需要程度(1-10)	價錢範圍
Mobile	10	3500-12000 HKD
Computer	8	3500-12000 HKD
Internet Fees	10	300-500 HKD
Apps	7	100-300 HKD Monthly
Web Systerm	7	300-700 HKD Monthly
Tripod	5	100-200 HKD Monthly
Microphone	6	100-300 HKD
Camera	5	3000-13000 HKD
Memory Card	5	100-300 HKD
USB Cable	5	100-300 HKD

The price is for reference only.
According to your needs, product brand, where you are located, and product quality may vary, thus changing the costs.

Myth #5: Does an online business run automatically without taking care of it?

Many people think that online businesses do not need to take the time to manage it after establishing the systems, and that it will automatically operate and sell for them.

However, this is not the case.

Many people start an online business with this idea in mind. After they establish the online platform, they leave it alone. But as the days go by and they find that no transactions have taken place, they feel that the online space is not the way to be successful, and they have wasted their time and effort on their online business.

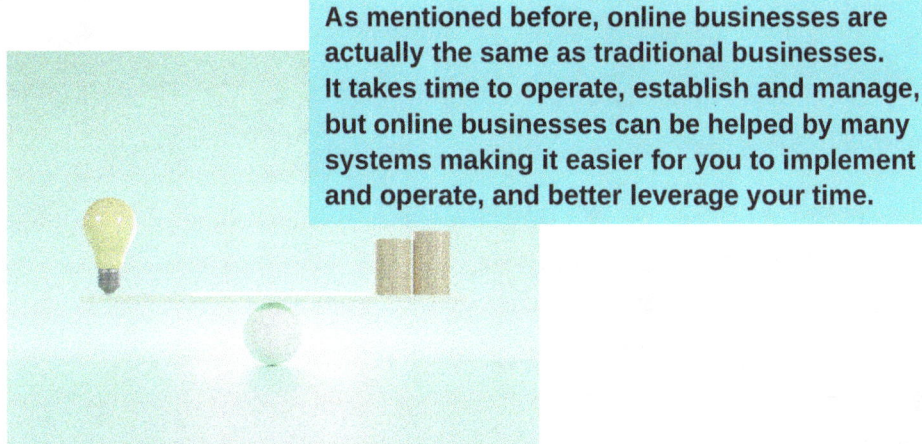

As mentioned before, online businesses are actually the same as traditional businesses. It takes time to operate, establish and manage, but online businesses can be helped by many systems making it easier for you to implement and operate, and better leverage your time.

When you first start an online business, you must allocate at least 2-3 hours a day to operate and manage the online platform.
The Step by Step guide in section 2 will explain in detail how you can operate and manage it.

Online businesses are actually the same as traditional businesses. It takes time to operate

Myth #6: Does An Online Business Make You Rich Overnight?

This idea is very wrong! No business will make you rich overnight.

You might say: "No, I saw in the news that there are those who gamble on Bitcoin, or sell NFTs, and they made more than a million overnight. Isn't this the power of online business?"

It should be said that no matter what, whether in the real world or the online world, there are very rare events that will make you rich overnight. Those who can make a lot of money in a short period of time from the Internet, you do not see the efforts behind them.

For example, it might take them a long time and in-depth research on the market before they develop/start, and spend a lot of time operating their own online platform daily until they have reached a large audience.

Online businesses proportionally allow you to make money faster than having a brick-and-mortar business, with lower overheads and allows you to profit faster, BUT it is important to build a strong foundation for your business. I will show you the foundation for building an online business in the Step By Step content.

No business will make you rich overnight

Step by Step to get started!

This chapter will guide you step by step to starting your online business!

Step 1: Select a "set" of platforms to get started

What is a "set" of platforms?

Online businesses must have a "promotion platform" and "sales platform", both are indispensable! Just like any brick-and-mortar stores and businesses, you need a good location to attract people and at the same time you need a store to sell your products.

When many people first start their online busines they only focus on the "sales platform". They spen a lot of time, effort and money just focusing o building a sales platform.

You may have a perfect platform with great desig and systems inside, but what about getting peop to your platform?

It's like when you have a perfectly designed store, hire the best staff, but no traffic and no traffic equals no sales... So, today I'm going to teach you how to choose a "set" of platforms to start your online business.

Promotion Platforms

The promotional platforms are to reach out to your potential customers, to build your brand, so that more people know and understand your products or services better.
It is very important to choose the right promotion platform, because this platform is the key to reaching customers.

How to choose a promotional platform?

As time passes, different types of promotional platforms may be added.
(Maybe Facebook may have been replaced by the time you are reading this article today). As times change, these platforms will continue to appear and disappear, just like the following platforms such as ICQ -> Messenger -> Facebook, to Snapchat, Twitter, etc., there may be more metaverse platforms and virtual world stores in the future...

With so many different types of promotional platforms, how do we choose? There will be different promotional platforms in the future, so is it necessary to switch platforms all the time? Do we need to keep up to date with the latest?

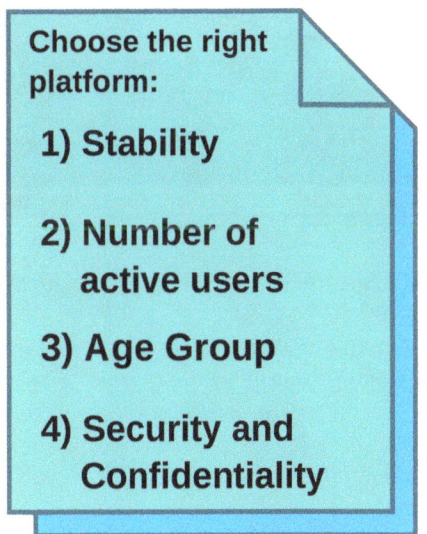

Choose the right platform:

1) Stability

2) Number of active users

3) Age Group

4) Security and Confidentiality

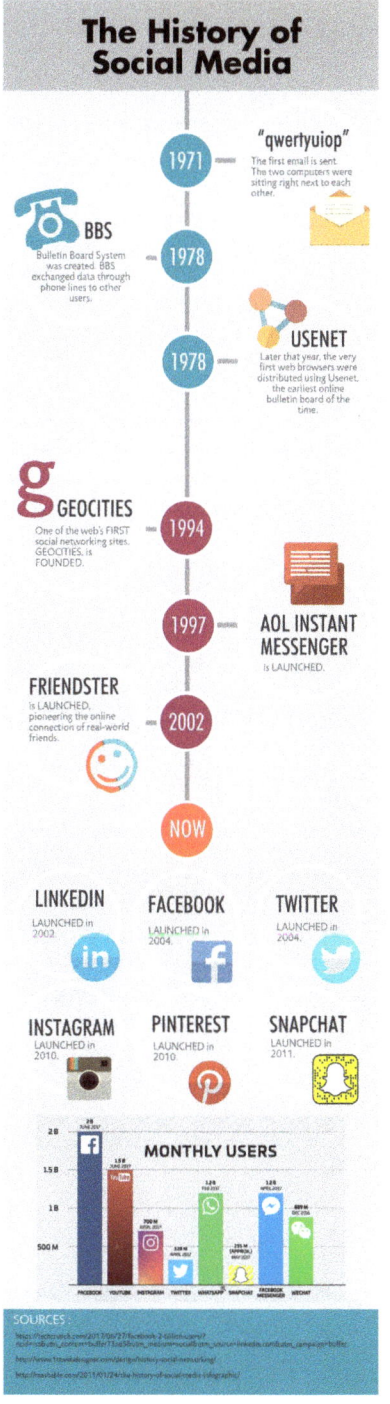

The History of Social Media

1971 — "qwertyuiop" The first email is sent. The two computers were sitting right next to each other.

BBS — Bulletin Board System was created. BBS exchanged data through phone lines to other users. — 1978

1978 — USENET Later that year, the very first web browsers were distributed using Usenet, the earliest online bulletin board of the time.

g GEOCITIES One of the web's FIRST social networking sites, GEOCITIES, is FOUNDED. — 1994

1997 — AOL INSTANT MESSENGER is LAUNCHED.

FRIENDSTER is LAUNCHED, pioneering the online connection of real-world friends. — 2002

NOW

LINKEDIN LAUNCHED in 2002.

FACEBOOK LAUNCHED in 2004.

TWITTER LAUNCHED in 2004.

INSTAGRAM LAUNCHED in 2010.

PINTEREST LAUNCHED in 2010.

SNAPCHAT LAUNCHED in 2011.

MONTHLY USERS

SOURCES :

1) Stability

First of all, we need to observe and analyze whether this promotional platform is stable or
not. Will it be disconnected for a day or two, unable to log in, information loss, etc.
If the platform is unstable, it will affect the flow of traffic and it will cause the loss of customers. Because of the instability of the platform, there will be possibilities of loss of time on the efforts you have put in on the articles or videos that you have worked hard to promote.

Therefore, when choosing a platform, you can spend a little time collecting information first,
but if you are really urgent, it is recommended to choose a platform that has existed for a while and has a stable number of people (such as Facebook) to start the first step.

JAN 2022
THE WORLD'S MOST-USED SOCIAL PLATFORMS
RANKING OF SOCIAL MEDIA PLATFORMS BY GLOBAL ACTIVE USER FIGURES (IN MILLIONS)

GLOBAL OVERVIEW

Platform	Users (millions)
FACEBOOK[1]	2,910
YOUTUBE[2]	2,562
WHATSAPP[1]*	2,000
INSTAGRAM[3]	1,478
WECHAT[1]	1,263
TIKTOK[4]	1,000
FB MESSENGER[2]	988
DOUYIN[4]	600
QQ[1]	574
SINA WEIBO[1]	573
KUAISHOU[1]	573
SNAPCHAT[1]	557
TELEGRAM[1]	550
PINTEREST[1]	444
TWITTER[3]	436
REDDIT[1]*	430
QUORA[1]*	300

99

SOURCES: KEPIOS ANALYSIS OF EL COMPANY ANNOUNCEMENTS OF MONTHLY ACTIVE USERS (2) USERS (NOTE THAT MONTHLY ACTIVE USER FIGURES MAY BE HIGHER). **ADVISORY:** USERS MAY NOT BE UPDATED USER FIGURES IN THE PAST 12 MONTHS, SO FIGURES ARE LESS REPRESENTATIVE. BASE:CHAT

資料来源: Hootsuite

2) Number of active users

We use the promotional platform because we need traffic. When choosing a platform
we need to pay attention to the number of users of the platform, as well as the **number of active users.**

Many platforms may have existed for a long time, although there is stability and
a large number of registered users, this platform may no longer be active.
(For example, many large discussion forums have a large number of users, but their activity is not as active as before.)

Age Demographics of Social Media Users

3) Age Group

Each promotional platform has a certain age group of users (for example, Facebook is about 25-55 years old, Snapchat is 13-20 years old) , you must first understand who and the age of your current product/service you want to promote to.

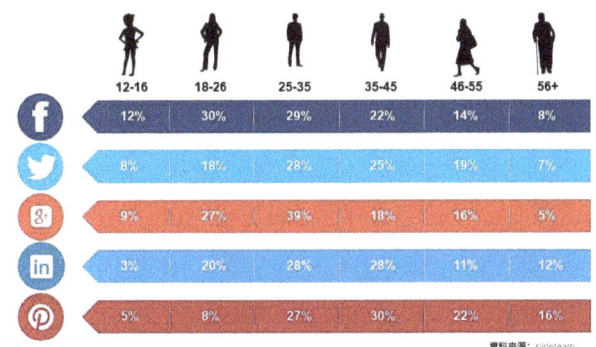

資料來源: slideteam

The easiest way to analyze the age group is to see which age group have purchased from you previously.

Usually, we divide the age group into 5 or 10 year groups (15-20 years old, or 25-35 years old), but remember the age group has to have purchasing power.

For example if the target customer of your product/service are children aged 5-10, you will not go to a platform that has children to promote, because the buyers are parents. We need to find the age group of the parents who have the ability to buy, and then analyze which platform they are active on.

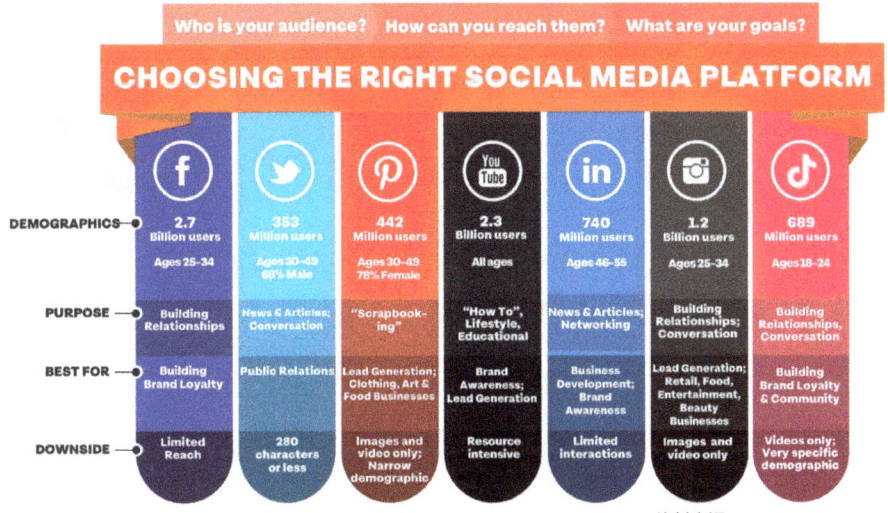

資料來源: aofung.org

4) Security and Confidentiality

Online security and confidentiality is the most important part for your customers. You must ensure that the promotional platform you choose has sufficient security systems and confidentiality clauses to protect your own information and customers information.

Generally, the current promotion platforms (Facebook, Youtube, etc.) have a good and stable system, such as two-factor authentication login. Although the online world is still full of a crisis of hackers and information leakage (even big banks have had data leakage incidents), some things we may not be able to fully control, but can be avoided as much as possible, so choose an established platform that has a secure system.

Some things we may not be able to fully control, but can be avoided as much as possible, so choose an established platform that has a secure system.

Sales platform

The sales platform is a channel to let customers buy your products/services, which is equivalent to the storefront and payment system of the physical store.

When customers notice your product/service from the promotion platform, the next step is, of course, to check your product to see if it is suitable and then buy it. And the customer's needs are actually very simple, they want a fast and direct purchase!

Customers have been attracted to your products from the promotion platform, so a good sales platform is not to explain the product in more detail, but to have a complete and smooth system for customers to simply buy the products you promote.

3 Key point of Sales platform:

Security

Payment System

User Friendliness

How to choose a sales platform?

1) User Friendliness

When choosing a sales platform, it is not only beneficial to choose one that is easy for us as the business owner to operate and use, but also needs to be very user friendly for customers. The system should be simple and smooth to lead customers to purchase successfully.

If the customer needs to find out how to buy, or if they need to join a member/establish a user to buy, it is too complicated, which will reduce the customer's desire to buy and lose this sales opportunity.

When choosing a sales platform, use it from the customer's point of view to see if it is convenient to use and the purchase process is simple.

Popular Sales Systerm

2) Payment System

The payment systems supported by various sales platforms are different, depending on the payment method used by your company, or the payment method used by the public, such as credit card, Paypal, etc.

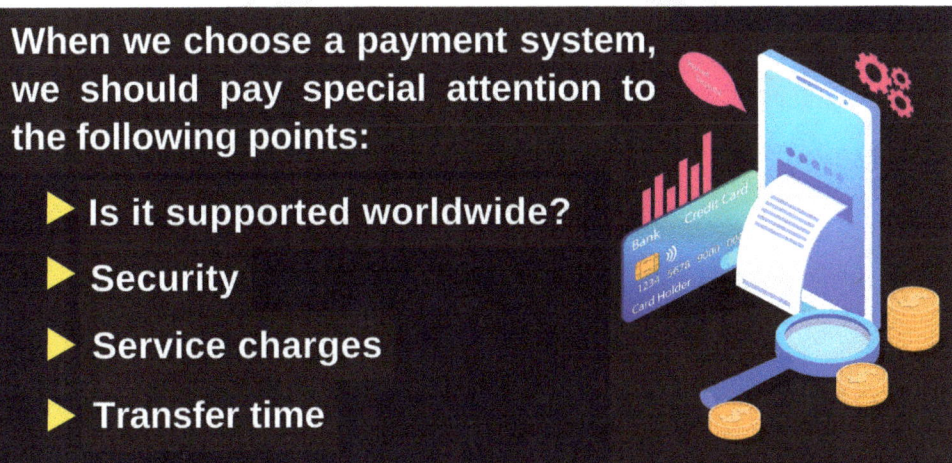

When we choose a payment system, we should pay special attention to the following points:

▶ **Is it supported worldwide?**

▶ **Security**

▶ **Service charges**

▶ **Transfer time**

When it involves money transactions and personal information, we must pay great attention to security, especially when there is news on the Internet about online scams or charging errors etc. A secure payment system for customers to buy with confidence is crucial.

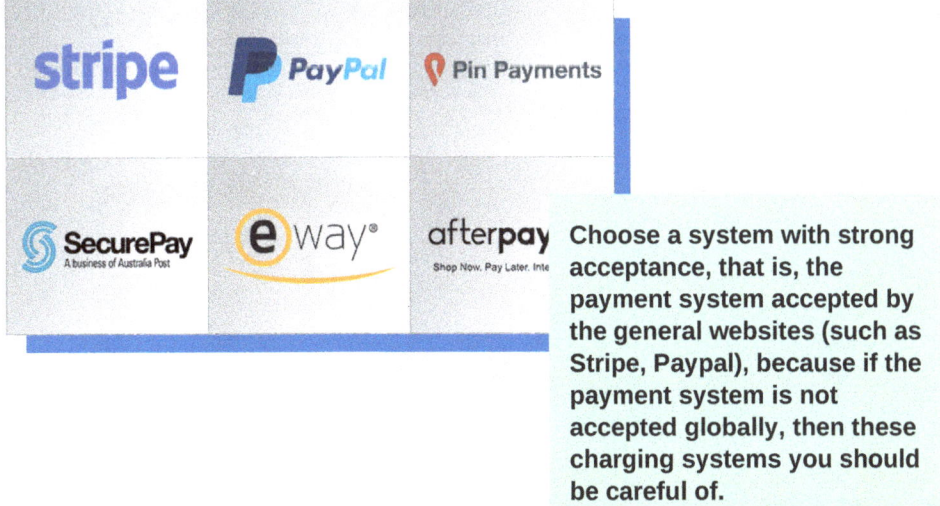

Choose a system with strong acceptance, that is, the payment system accepted by the general websites (such as Stripe, Paypal), because if the payment system is not accepted globally, then these charging systems you should be careful of.

3) Security

The sales platform, in addition to money transactions, (depending on different product types) some of us will collect customer information such as email, phone, etc

Therefore, the security of the entire sales platform is very important. Although there are many free sales platforms in the market, it is very important to choose a platform that guarantees both parties, which will be directed related to the customer's trust in you.

Once the customer's data is lost due to choosing the wrong platform, your hard-earned online business may also be greatly affected.

Step 2: Start Up Basic Equipment

To conduct an online business, like any business, you must prepare basic equipment to start smoothly, just like if you want to open a restaurant, basic equipment such as kitchen, dishes, stools, etc.

1) Smartphone

Although everyone has a mobile phone or a smartphone now, not every mobile phone is suitable for the software (Apps) or systems required for online business. To facilitate your online business, it is recommended to simply upgrade the mobile phone first, such as a newer model, with increased capacity, faster speed and clear lens pixels (this is very important, because videos and photos are an important part of promoting products).

2) Computer

We can now handle a lot of things on the phone, so many people don't use computers anymore, but if you want to start an online business, a computer is really important. Because there are many settings in the promotional platforms and sales platforms that can only be modified on the computer. The system processing of the mobile phone has not completely replaced the computer. According to your own needs, you do not necessarily need a very advanced computer. At present, the general word processing computer is sufficient, and in the future, it will be gradually upgraded according to the usage or demand.

3) Tripod (for filming)

Because you have to make videos frequently, a tripod will make the stability and angle of the video look more professional. Because many people do not think of buying a tripod at the beginning, when shooting with a mobile phone with their hands free, the video would become blurred because the hand would move, making the video unattractive. Or you can't find a place to put your mobile phone at home to shoot, and the angle is too high or too low, which will reduce the quality of the video.

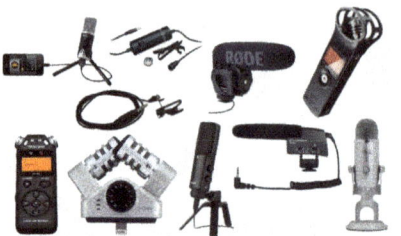

4) Microphone

To build on the promotional platform, videos and live broadcasts are necessary, so I set the microphone as a basic device. You don't need to buy a very professional one. Find one that is able to pick up the sound closely and isolate some noise, and that should be sufficient.

Step 3: Be courageous and wise to build your platform

Don't be afraid, be brave and click around

You don't need to be an IT genius to start an online business, but you need to have a brave mentality and be willing to try.

When you are just starting out on your online business journey, and you are unfamiliar, you may be afraid to click other steps, due to fear that the computer will be broken or the whole system will be wrong if you click randomly. In fact, pressing in to view every step or every setting will not break the system, so be brave and take a look at the setting on the platform to understand the location of the settings, or what function you may have. After using it, if there is a function that is not understood, there will usually be a circle (i) or (?) pattern next to it. Click it and you will see the instructions.

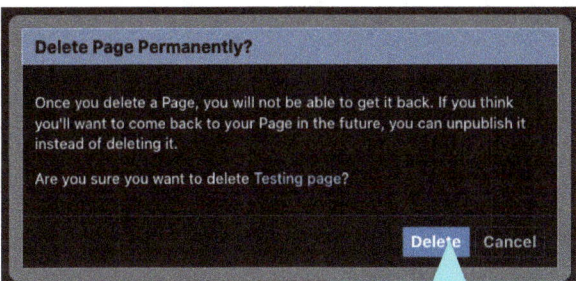

Delete Page Permanently?

Once you delete a Page, you will not be able to get it back. If you think you'll want to come back to your Page in the future, you can unpublish it instead of deleting it.

Are you sure you want to delete Testing page?

Delete   Cancel

One of the advantages of exploring a new platform at the beginning is if you mess up and select all the wrong settings, you can abandon the page and build it again. Because the page has just been established, even if you restarted it will not affect you too much.

If your platform has been established for a while, and then you click the wrong settings on the platform because you don't know the platform, then it will be a big loss to start all over again.

**Be courageous and publish posts,
carefully paying attention to the response.**

As part of your online business journey it is indispensable for "promotion", and establishing authority on the promotional platform requires a lot of valuable content to attract potential customers.

But what content do your customers like? Stop here for a moment...
Don't think too deeply, otherwise your first post will never be published...
Let's be courageous and publish your first post, the suggestion is the self-introduction category,
such as telling your own story , or the company's philosophy, etc.

It takes time to build traction on the promotional platform, and each post is a brick for building your authority. At least one brick (one post) should be built every day. If you think too much, the speed of building a platform will slow down.

First, make different types of posts courageously, so that you can get used to the feeling of posting. At the same time, pay attention to the reaction of the audience on the platform to see which types of posts are more attractive, and then set the ratio of this type of posts. The steps later will teach you simple data analysis and promotion methods.

Believing in your uniqueness

Not only do you need to be courageous to post, but also be confident in expressing yourself and creating your own uniqueness.

When we first start to build a promotional platform, we more or less use other people's posting methods, but after getting used to the process of posting, we must create our own uniqueness or insist on our own uniqueness.

To build a relationship of trust with customers, express yourself sincerely, because customers buy the products and services you promote because they believe in you.

So, be courageous and confident and express in your own way and believe in your uniqueness!

Step 4: Time allocation for promotion, management and operation.

Promotional methods

Selling your products/services on the promotional platform can be simply classified into the following promotion methods.

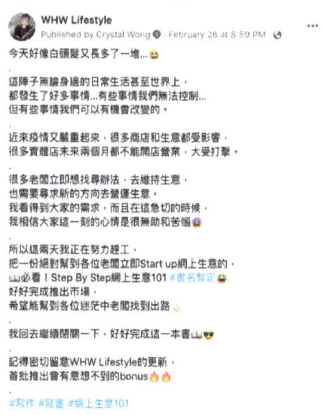

1) Text Content

Use attractive copywriting to bring out the story the product so that potential customers can lear more about your product, and then lead them to th sales platform.

The advantage of text content is that you can brin out some more detailed information from the tex allowing customers to understand more deeply.

However, the disadvantage is that if the content o the text is too long it may cause customers to sto reading, and because the text is difficult to conve emotions, the effect will be lower than that of video and live broadcasts.

2) Image Content

Simple and beautiful images can instantly grab the attention of potential customers stopping to check out the informational content of your promotion.

The advantage of using images to promote is that customers can immediately pay attention to the key points brought out (the effect will vary according to the design layout).

A customer might respond to the images of the product, they can proceed to make a purchase (such as pictures of clothes and shoes)

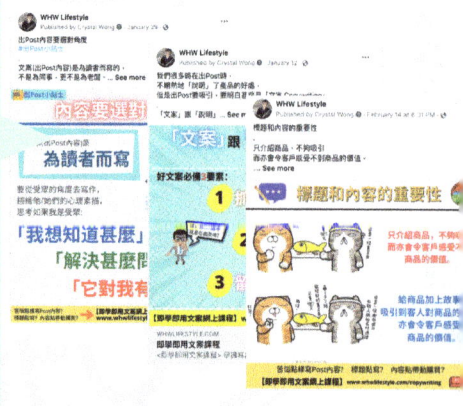

However the disadvantage of images is that you can't put too much information in the image content, and sometimes the simplified focus may not fully bring out what you want to express. Therefore, many times we will combine images and text content to improve the effect.

Text is the soul of all promotional content. Even for video content, you must know how to start with text first. Therefore, you must have certain skills in writing text content in order to attract customers and drive the motivation to buy.I have designed a copywriting online course, which will teach you in more depth on how to write words that can "sell" from the title to the content.
Learn More: **www.whwlifestyle.com/copywriting**

3) Video content

Video content can be said to be a necessary method for promotion, because video content can perfectly express in ways that pictures and texts cannot, so that potential customers can absorb the information more deeply.

The sound and image will bring us more emotional feelings, for example, when you want to bring out the story behind the brand, you will tell it in person, and the feeling will be deeper. If there are only words, it may be able to bring emotions, but it is certainly not as deep as video.

The disadvantage of the video is that it takes time to produce and edit, and the content layout also requires careful planning. If you are not familiar with filming, the content of the film will be more difficult. I suggest taking some filming courses and content writing courses so that you can be more efficient in producing video content.

4) Live Streaming Interactive Promotion

Live Streaming is one of the best ways to **build trust and long-term relationships with customers**. Customers have direct access to you (a real person), making them understand and trust you better. At the same time, you can also watch the reactions of customers in real time, understand their preferences and so on. The advantage of live broadcast is that it can be done for a long time, which is convenient to bring out some information categories that need to be explained in detail. Of course, it can also conduct activities that interact with customers, such as Q&A, etc.

The downside of live streaming is that it definitely requires a stable network, as intermittent stagnation can prevent customers from watching.

Many people find that to live broadcast you will need to overcome the psychological barrier. You will need to interact directly with unfamiliar customers, so many people who are new to online businesses are afraid to use live broadcasts to promote.

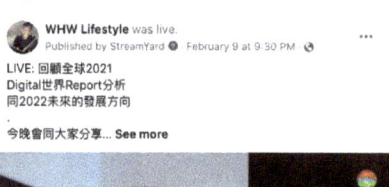

I'm here to give you a live broadcast tip, "Want to broadcast live? Just press the live button to start!" At the beginning, don't worry about whether there are people watching or not. All you have to do is try a live broadcast. If you feel that the content is not very good during the live broadcast, you can just pause and delete the video, don't worry too much. The more you practice live streaming, the more you'll be ready by the time you've actually got a large number of people watching throughout the day! (If you are never ready, and suddenly a large number of viewers, it will not only surprise you, but also may cause the loss of customers due to mistakes).

Filming and live streaming is not as difficult as you think, as long as you learn the skills. It is easy to get started.
I designed a 5-day [1 Take Filming Online Course], which will teach you how to overcome camera fear, how to arrange content and time, etc. in the simplest way. If anyone is interested you can go to the following website:
www.whwlifestyle.com/onetakevideo

Management and Time Allocation of your online business

Online business management is a little easier than physical stores, but it is still necessary to work hard and know how to allocate time to manage, otherwise many people encounter the following problems::

1) The development of online platforms is slow due to the allocation of too little time

2) Feeling overwhelmed by adding extra online operations to an already full schedule.

I divide an online business into management projects and business projects so it's a lot easier when you're dealing with and allocating your time.

Management

In terms of management, there is not much to manage on an online business. After getting used to it, it can be completed in about 1 hour a day (it also depends on the size of your platform). The list to manage is as follows:

1) Interaction with the potential customers on the promotional platform (replying to comments, messages, etc.)

2) Analyzing data (such as the performance of the promoted post)

3) Processing orders

4) Customer service

It is recommended to set 2-3 hours a day to deal with the above things when you first start. When the online business is a bit more established with procedures, the above things would be easier to manage, or you could hire someone to take over. (It is best to understand the whole process by yourself before you start to hire someone.)

Business operations

In terms of business operations, it takes more time and planning in advance, otherwise you will start to feel overwhelmed. Business projects are an important part of online business, including promotion and sales.

The list to be followed is as below:

1）Establish a promotion platform
(keep the promotion platform updated, such as text and image posts, live broadcast, video, etc.)

2）Set the promotion content
(continuing on the above point, you have to plan and set the promoted content)

3）Create the promotion content
(this part take the most time, so pre-planning is necessary)

4）Sales process
(if the promotion successfully attracts customers and leads to sales, the process of sales must be prepared in advance)

With these items, it is best to plan in advance before you start implementing to make it relatively smooth.

It is recommended to spend one day a week to plan the content you are going to promote. The content setting direction can be from：

Products/Services Offering Discounts

Holiday Seasons

Brands/self-story Sharing

Examples/Successful Testimonial Sharing

Educational Content

Pure Sales Content

Having an outline on the content and planning a promotional timetable is necessary.
It is recommended to maintain one promotional post a day, but if you are not used to it
at the beginning or if you run out of time with your promotional items, maintain at least
one promotional post a week. It is necessary to keep the promotion platform updated
so that customers can notice it.

WEEKLY SOCIAL MEDIA PLAN

Designed By

Crystal Wong
WHW LIFESTYLE

(Month: **1月**)

Thing to Focus — New Product Launch — Increase Sales
— CNY

monday	tuesday	wednesday	thursday	friday	saturday	sunday
節日季節	教學資訊分享	品牌/自身故事分享	實例/成功例子分享	純銷售內容		產品/服務推出優惠

下載高清Weekly Social Media Plan：https://bit.ly/3IGmP5Z

**Once you have an approximate timetable
for promotion, you must arrange time to
produce the required promotional
content, such as the copywriting for the
text content, video production, or live
broadcast preparation.**

How to handle massive content production?

I will divide the preparation content into 3 levels

Level 3
Takes time to prepare, but don't delay for too long otherwise you may procrastinate and "slow" completion, and miss the best time to launch this promotion.

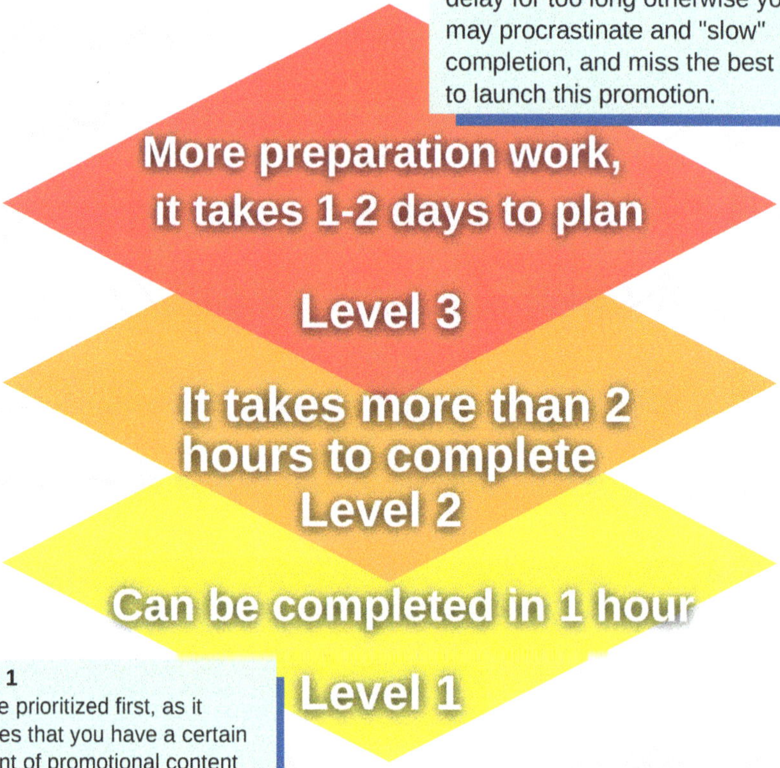

More preparation work, it takes 1-2 days to plan

Level 3

It takes more than 2 hours to complete
Level 2

Can be completed in 1 hour

Level 1

Level 1
can be prioritized first, as it ensures that you have a certain amount of promotional content ready.

Level 2
complete it within one day if time permits in the schedule.It is best not to divide the Level 2 category for more than two days. These contents, such as videos, may be shot very smoothly when inspiration emerges, but unfortunately, it will be more difficult to record once the inspiration passes.

Step 5: Sales process design and customer experience

"Promoting" your online business is a front end step, responsible for attracting customers to buy, but to make customers complete the purchase or increase the purchase amount/quantity, you need a back end system, then that would complete the sale!

Selling is reminiscent of having a salesperson explain your product to you and then persuade you to buy it. However, in an online business, it is not possible to hire a "salesperson" for each product independently, so how do we sell it?

In online sales, we don't necessarily need a salesperson. What you need is a complete sales process. (If you are selling products in the service category, you may need a sales team to contact customers).

ONLINE SHOPPING

What is a sales process?

The sales process is that after the customer enters your online "shop" from the promotion platform, the "promoted product" leads the customer to purchase additional products, and then recommends the purchase of a one-time special offer.

The main purpose of the whole sales process is to increase the purchase amount of customers to increase the total sales amount made. The above is just one example of the sales process. According to different business models and product types, the design of the sales process can be very diversified.

The following are some basic sales process design examples for reference:

Physical product sales process:
Main product -> additional matching products or add more purchases -> more discounts (Optional)

Service based sales process:
Appointment service- > Promote additional service discounts or matching products -> Promote or sell more advanced services

Online courses Sales process:
Introductory courses -> Limited time Bonus -> Next-level courses or VIP services

The products and services provided by each business are unique, so the sales process cannot be designed only with one of the templates. For example, physical products and online courses can also complement each other in the sales process.

If you need assistance in designing the sales process and sales system, you can make an appointment with me for a one-to-one free consultation, let me understand your business model, products and services, and then plan the most suitable sales process for your business and design your own sales system.
www.whwlifestyle.com/call

Customer Experience

A smooth sales process can greatly enhance the customer experience.

You may have experienced this yourself after seeing the promoted advertisement and then you were attracted to a certain store to buy the product. When you encountered a question but the salesperson couldn't help, the system was slow and malfunctioned when making payment. Maybe you have put the product in the cart and didn't buy it. Maybe you still bought the product, but the whole buying experience did not leave a good impression...
You probably won't go back to buy it again, and you won't introduce it to your friends because of the bad experience.

So, when designing the sales process, we don't want to just focus on the sales amount or the most expensive product, we need to design from the customer's point of view. For example, if you are promoting skin products, after the customer puts the skin essence into the shopping cart,

What else do you sell next?

A) Can it be used in combination with a night cream that can achieve better results?

B) Or sell unrelated premium UV protection sleeves?

Both can increase sales, but customers will want you to understand their needs better and provide them with the best solution/product/service.

It's like when you go to a store, you take a promotional product, and a salesperson comes to you to understand and recommend additional products that are suitable for you,
and then guide you through a fast and smooth payment system. The entire purchase process is very smooth, and you as the purchaser had a great experience. You will buy from this store again in the future, and will also introduce it to your friends.

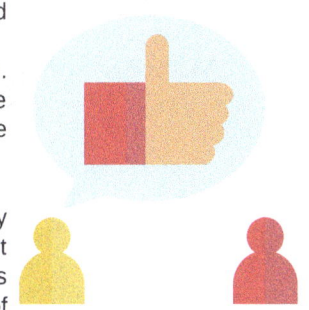

Customer experience is related to whether customers will buy from you again in the future, or whether they will recommend it to friends around you. Designing a set of experience processes that are exclusive to your customers can increase the rate of customers returning to purchase.

Step 6: How to simply analyze data and get the latest information?

Analyzing data allows us to know whether the results of our promotion and sales are up to expectations, and also allows us to understand where we need to improve and do better. There are many types of data, and some can be studied more in depth, but today we will analyze the data that immediately helps us understand your online business.

The data that needs to be understood is to know whether the promoted content has reached the target customers, and other basic data analysis:

Reach

Number of Views

Number of Likes

Contact reach rate represents how many people your promoted content has reached, but this data does not mean that they have watched your content, this data can only mean that your promoted content has appeared on their platform. (The reach rate is not under our control, but is affected by the algorithm of the promotion platform you use.)

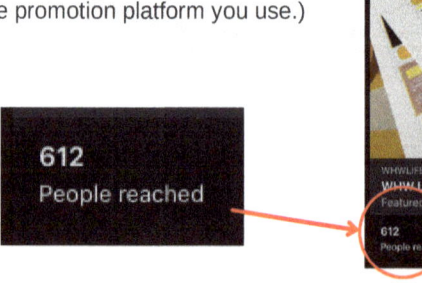

To know whether the promotional content attracts the right customers to watch, it is necessary to analyze the data of the number of views.

If the **number of views** is more than 30% of the reach rate, this is a good performance, and a higher percentage means that the promoted content is exactly the category that customers like.。

The data of the **number of likes** is to see whether the relationship between you and the customer is close or not. However, now the number of likes cannot be used to absolutely determine the popularity of the promoted content, because many people do not want to move their fingers to like. Therefore, the likes can only be used as a superficial reference. Don't be discouraged by the low data, because we focus on the success rate of the final sale.

The data we are most concerned about is of course the sales success rate, because even if the promoted content is very attractive for customers to watch and like, what we want is for customers to successfully purchase the product.

After collecting the data from the promoted content for a month, see how many successful sales are in this month.

For example, the contact rate of the promoted content is 100, the number of views is 50, and the number of purchases is 10, then your purchase success rate is 20%

$$\frac{\text{The number of purchases}}{\text{View Rate}}\ \% = \text{The Purchase Success Rate}$$

The above is just a calculation method for simple analysis, which is enough to know whether the content of promotion and the results of sales from that particular promotion.

For example, in-depth calculation methods include contact rate, sales process contact data, advertising costs, customer repurchase data, etc., which will not be discussed in depth here, because the data calculation can be deep enough to explain in its own online course.

How can I get the latest news?

There is a lot of information on the Internet daily. Even if you don't need to keep up with every new reporting regarding technology, you should at least have a little understanding of the new direction of the future, so that you can prepare and plan, or just match your business development.

To get the latest information, you can follow some platforms or companies that provide new information (for example, you can pay attention to our WHW Lifestyle page on various platforms), or check the latest technology news on Google. If you want to know a specific range, you can search for keywords in the range to get up-to-date information.

Be in front of your competition by understanding the market before your competitors

Make watching the latest news as one of the daily tasks, because once we come into contact with online business, we need to know the external situations all the time, and be faster than your competitors to understand the future development and plan the preparations now.

Summarize

Action!!

Take action!

To start your online business, the first step is taking action!

Many people continue to read materials or study, although it is a good thing, but if they do not put into practice what they have learned, it will be a waste.

Hopefully when you learn how to start your online business, Get started now!

Stop hesitating because when you stop to think,
A lot of people, even your competitors, are already doing it.

Online business is a necessary development direction in the future, so take the first step quickly, open your online market, and set off towards a more prosperous future!

You've got this and I support you always!

Thank you for reading this book, and I hope the information I have given you will get you started on your online business journey!

I would like to share some of my experiences here, and some of the problems my client have faced. Hope these experiences will give you a better understanding of online business and don't worry if you encounter the same problem.

When I first set up my online business, the process at the beginning is never as smooth as I imagined, which is absolutely normal, but I am impatient, so when one method did not work, I immediately changed and try another method, but the change was too fast I didn't give these methods a chance to settle and grow, which made the online business direction very confusing at the beginning, and customers didn't know what it was promoting. So don't make the same mistake as me. Online business is like growing vegetables. You have to run it slowly before you can see the harvest. Don't be impatient!

As mentioned above, online business is like farming vegetables, but different varieties of vegetables grow at different speeds. Some vegetables can be harvested in 2-3 weeks, and some vegetables can be harvested in 3 months. Because everyone's planting is different (products/services/promotion methods are different), we will see the harvest as long as we manage the present well, and we must persevere and don't give up! Farming take time to see, but they grow very quickly when they emerge. This is the law of nature and this analogy can also be used in an online business.

I would like to share the situation encountered by one of the customers. He spent more than 2 years establishing his own online business. He slowly developed his own way and promotion method, and also attracted the support of customers who followed his ideas, but because of this, he became too busy, and there is less live broadcast on the promotion platform. In just 2 months, the customer contact rate and viewing rate had dropped significantly. So, I hope everyone persists and continues building their own online business every day. The online world is developing very fast and people are very forgetful. If you don't interact with your customers, people will soon forget you. Be a step ahead of the competitors.

Finally, I would like to thank my family and friends who have always supported me behind my back, and my father and mother who allowed me to start my online business journey, even though they didn't know what it was, they still supported me. Many thanks to my partner, who has always supported my career development without complaint, and still doesn't blame me for being so busy sometimes that I don't have time to cook, haha. I would also like to express my special thanks to my Owl Buddy for her support. Without her support, this book would not exist today. I am so grateful and honoured to know her.

I also sincerely thank you for purchasing this book and for supporting me!
Without your support, WHW Lifestyle would not continue to serve you!

Here, I send my best wishes.
I hope your online business will develop beautifully,
so that your products/services can help more people.

Regards,
Crystal Wong

WHW Lifestyle

SALES FUNNEL EXPERT

www.whwlifestyle.com

whwlifestyle

whw.lifestyle

WHW Lifestyle